Voyage of the Kon-Tiki

Copyright © 1979, Macdonald-Raintree, Inc.

All rights reserved. No part of this book may be reproduced or utilized in any form or by any means, electronic or mechanical, including photocopying, recording, or by any information storage and retrieval system, without permission in writing from the Publisher. Inquiries should be addressed to Macdonald-Raintree, Inc., 205 West Highland Avenue, Milwaukee, Wisconsin 53203.

Library of Congress Number: 78-26766

1 2 3 4 5 6 7 8 9 0 83 82 81 80 79

Printed and bound in the United States of America.

Library of Congress Cataloging in Publication Data

Engel, Dolores.
   Voyage of the Kon-Tiki.

   SUMMARY: Describes the adventures of Thor Heyerdahl and his crew as they sail across the Pacific on the raft Kon-Tiki in an attempt to prove that the first Polynesian settlers could have come from South America.
   1. Heyerdahl, Thor — Juvenile literature. 2. Kon-Tiki Ekspedisjonen, 1947 — Juvenile literature.
3. Pacific Ocean — Juvenile literature. 4. Ethnology — Polynesia — Juvenile literature. [1. Kon-Tiki Expedition, 1947. 2. Heyerdahl, Thor] I. Bale, Gary. II. Title.
G530.H47E53   910'.92'4 [B]   78-26766
ISBN 0-8393-0151-0 lib. bdg.

Voyage of the Kon-Tiki

By
Dolores Engel

Illustrations by
Gary Bale

Raintree Publishers
Milwaukee • Toronto • Melbourne • London

Nobody knows for sure where the ancestors of the Polynesian people in the South Seas came from. Thor Heyerdahl believed that they had come from South America by raft about 1,500 years ago.

Thor, a young Norwegian, wanted to prove his idea. So he went to Peru in South America where he was joined by five other adventurers. Their names were Bengt, Erik, Herman, Knut, and Torstein. They planned to build a raft of balsa wood just like the ones used by the Indians who lived in South America hundreds of years ago. Then Thor and his crew were going to make the journey from Peru to the South Seas themselves.

It was hard to find balsa wood logs along the coast. So Thor and Herman traveled into the jungle of the Andes Mountains. As they went through the jungle, they met tribes of Indians. The men also saw snakes, scorpions, ants as large as scorpions, alligators, and giant lizards.

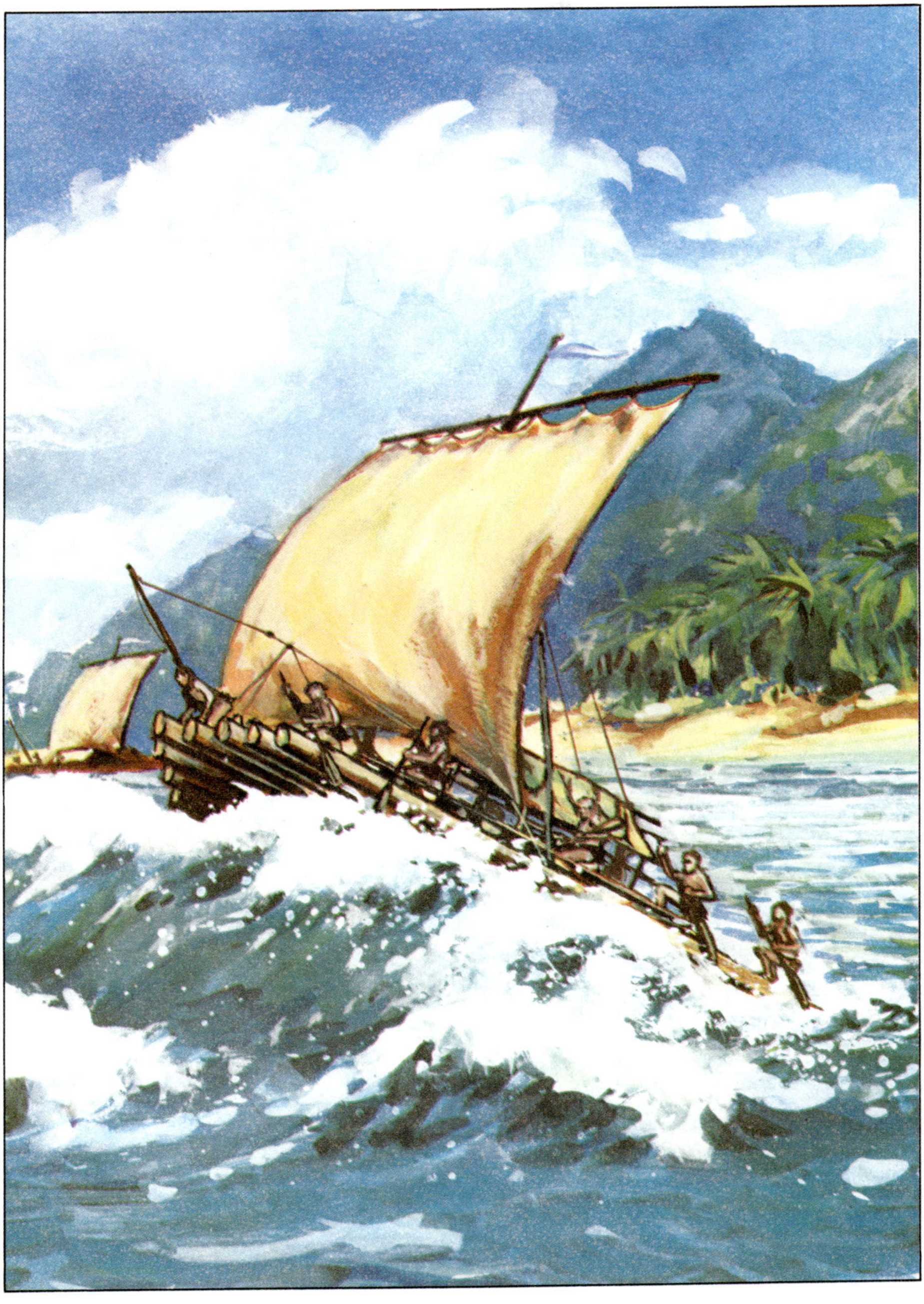

At last they found enough large trees. After cutting the trees down, the men lashed them together with tropical vines called lianas. Then Thor and Herman floated on their rough raft down the river toward the sea. Later the raft was taken by boat to the port of Callao in Peru. Here Thor and his crew would build the raft the same way the Indians had.

First the adventurers built a deck of split bamboo on top of the logs. Then they made a small, open cabin of bamboo canes with walls of braided bamboo leaves. Two masts of hard mangrove wood leaned towards each other and were tied at the top. A big square sail was attached to the masts.

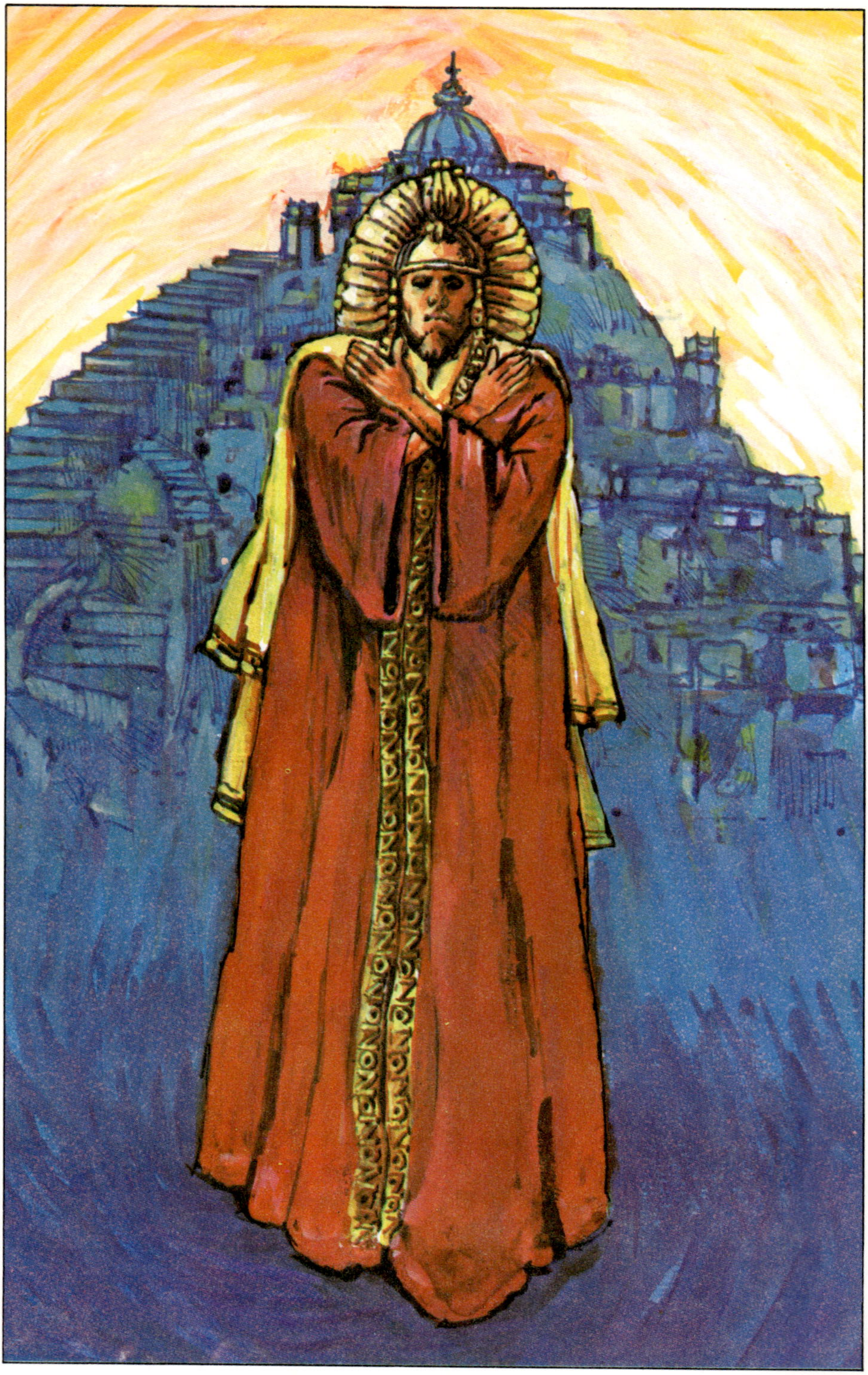

Thor and his crew called the raft *Kon-Tiki*. According to a legend, Kon-Tiki was a high priest and sun-king of people who had lived in Peru before the Incas. Kon-Tiki and his people had sailed west from the coast of Peru and were never seen there again. The Polynesian people living in the South Seas had a legend too. They believed that their ancestor-chief called Tiki had come to them from the east. Thor thought that Kon-Tiki and Tiki were the same person. To prove that the Indians long ago could have made such a voyage, Thor planned to make the same journey in the raft *Kon-Tiki*.

Just before the *Kon-Tiki* sailed, a well-wisher gave the adventurers a green parrot in a cage. The parrot was full of fun and often made the crew laugh. At first the parrot spoke only Spanish. But soon it learned some Norwegian words.

The explorers stored their supplies in cardboard boxes under the bamboo deck. They put their drinking water in small cans. The army had given them special survival food to test on the journey. Altogether, with baskets of fresh fruit and coconuts, they had enough supplies to last for four months. Besides food and water, they also took scientific instruments, cameras, radio equipment, a guitar, books, reed mats, and straw mattresses.

On April 28, 1947, a large crowd of people gathered to watch the *Kon-Tiki* set off westward across the Pacific.

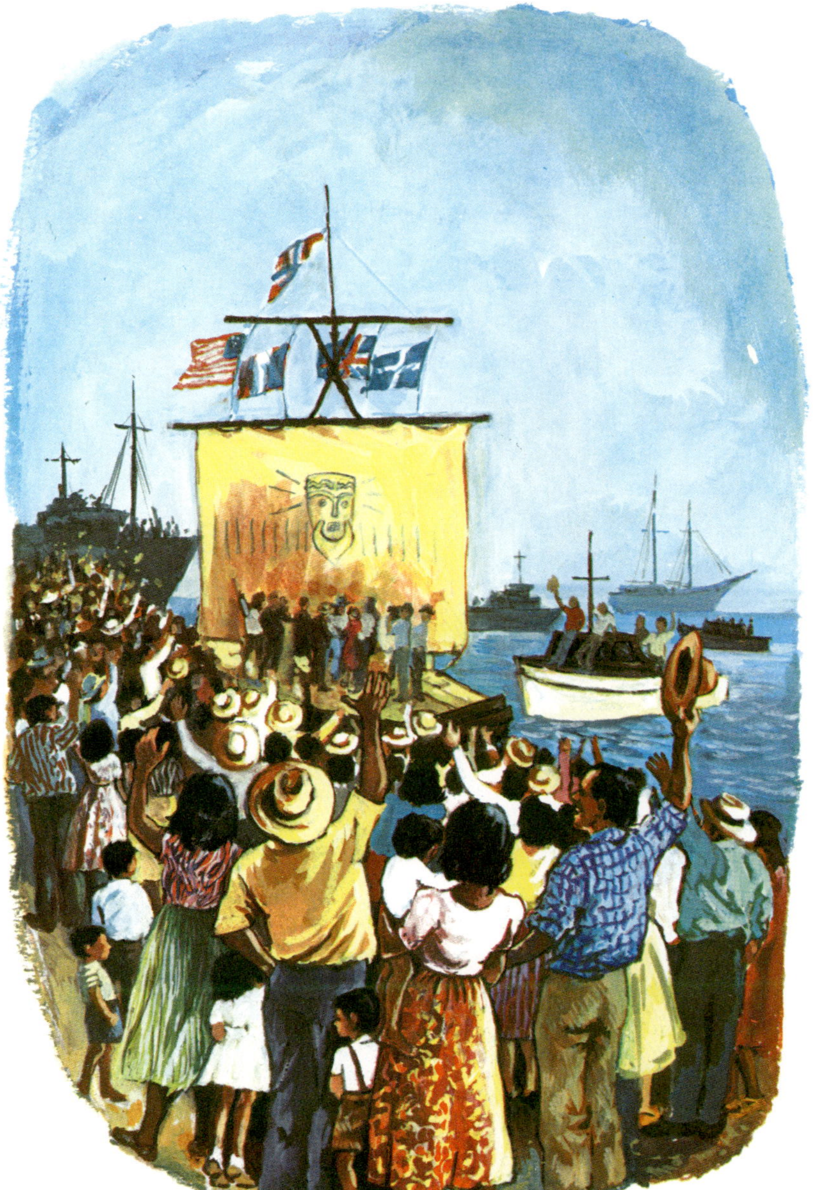

12

The *Kon-Tiki* was towed out of the harbor into the rough seas near the coast. Now the raft was at the mercy of the wind and waves. Soon it was in the swiftest part of the Humboldt Current, where strong winds carried it beyond where it could return. In the big waves, the *Kon-Tiki* bobbed about like a cork. A more modern boat might have turned over or been swamped. Near midnight, the adventurers sighted the last ship they would see on their voyage. Now they were alone with the sea.

Steering the raft in heavy seas was hard work. Two crew members at a time formed the steering watch at the heavy oar. When large waves broke over the raft, the men had to leap away from the oar and cling to the bamboo poles of the cabin roof. Then they had to leap back down and grab the oar before the raft began to turn. If the *Kon-Tiki* had turned around, it would have been difficult to turn it back again.

At first the men wondered if the raft would hold together. The soft logs soaked up water. Soon the raft floated lower in the water than it had at first. The logs heaved and groaned against the ropes that held them together. The crew checked the ropes daily. The men leaned over the edge of the raft with their heads under the water to inspect the ropes.

Flying fish constantly fell onto the raft. The crew either ate them or used them as bait to catch other fish or dolphins. There was never any danger of dying of hunger or thirst. The men could have survived on the water they got from chewing the raw fish. Sharks were daily visitors, and once the raft was nosed by a huge whale shark. At night the sea was phosphorescent. Sometimes the men looked down into the big shining eyes of deep-water fish.

So the weeks passed, with the *Kon-Tiki* pitching and rolling as it moved slowly westward. Often the sea was calm and smooth. But during storms, the helmsman would be up to his waist in water.

Occasionally two of the men would row out from the raft in the dinghy. One day, they found it very difficult to row back. The wind and waves kept carrying them away. After that, the dinghy was always attached to the *Kon-Tiki* by a long rope.

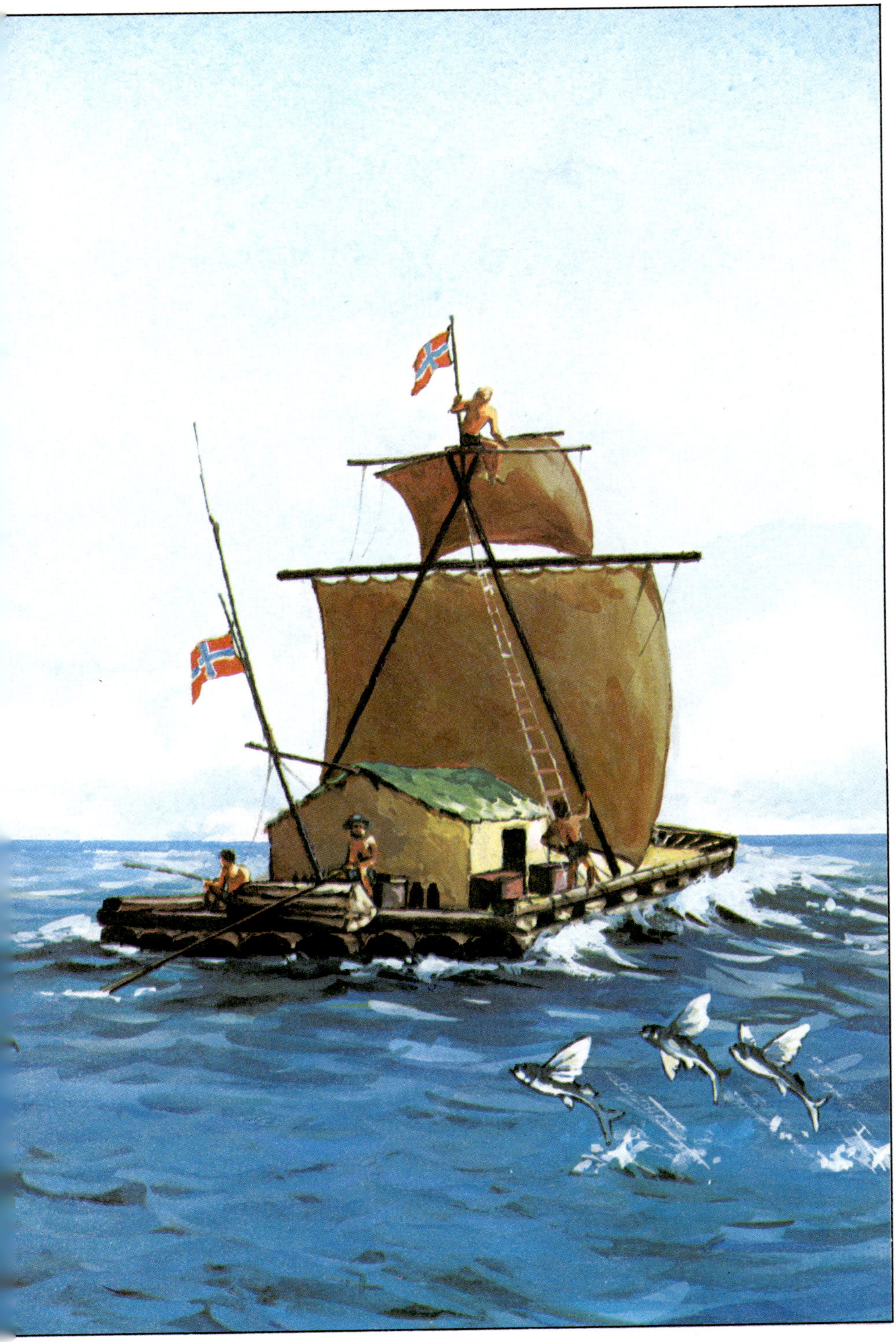

Once, as a storm was approaching, Torstein's sleeping bag was blown overboard. As Herman tried to grab it, he fell into the shark infested water. Because of the high waves, Herman could not swim back to the raft. Someone pushed the blade of the steering oar out to him. But he could not reach it. A life belt was thrown but it blew back to the raft before Herman could reach it.

Bengt and Thor went after him in the dinghy, but they could not reach him. From the raft Knut could see that Herman was drifting away. With a life belt in one hand, Knut dived from the raft and swam towards him. When Knut reached Herman, they both held onto the life belt. Then the other four crew members pulled them back to the raft. The sleeping bag floated in the distance for a little while and then was pulled under the surface by a large sea animal.

After two months at sea, the *Kon-Tiki* was still hundreds of miles from Polynesia. The raft was weaker and the ropes were gradually becoming looser. The logs were now covered with slippery weeds. The crew's drinking water and provisions were getting low. But the *Kon-Tiki* traveled slowly on.

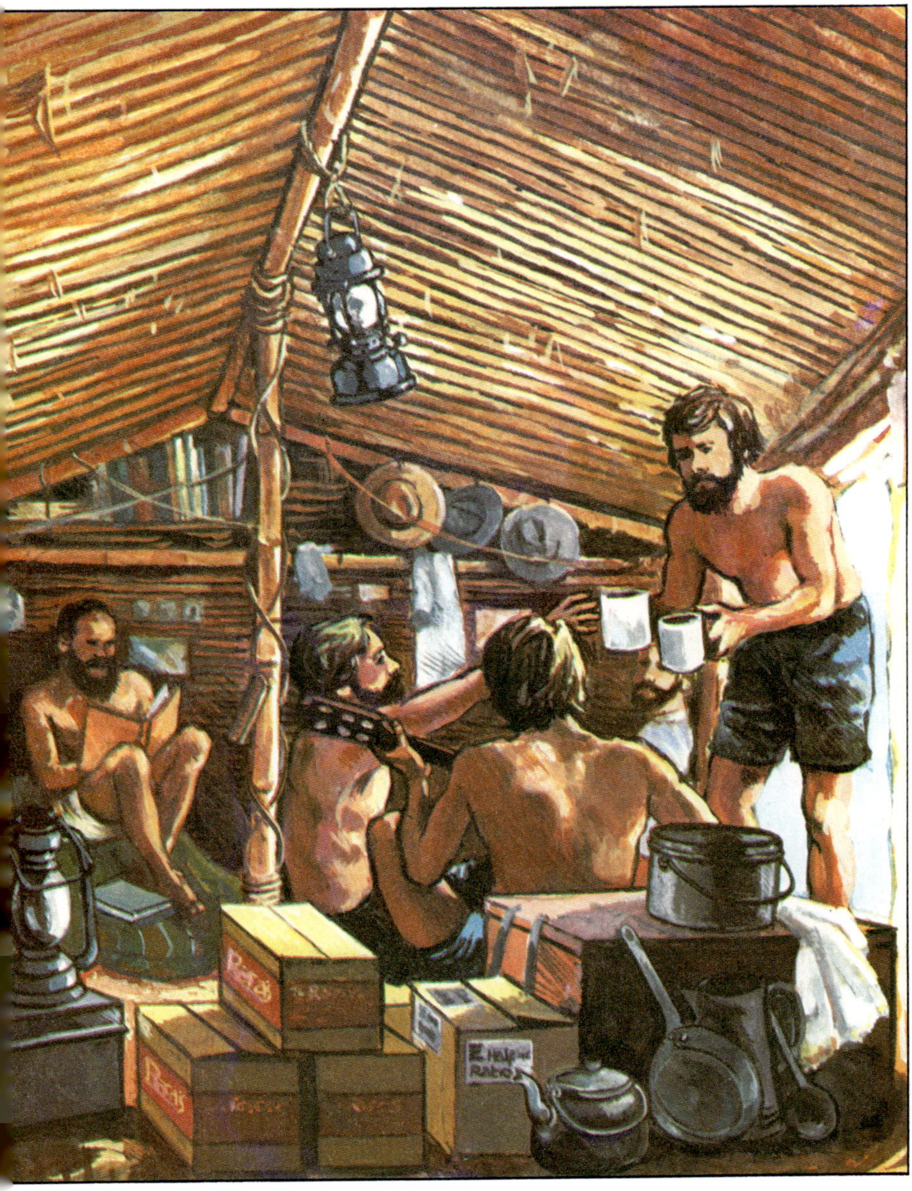

Soon the crew sighted some seabirds. So the men knew they must be nearing land at last. A few days later they came near an island. They saw a smoke signal rising in the air. But they drifted past the island because they could not steer the raft towards it.

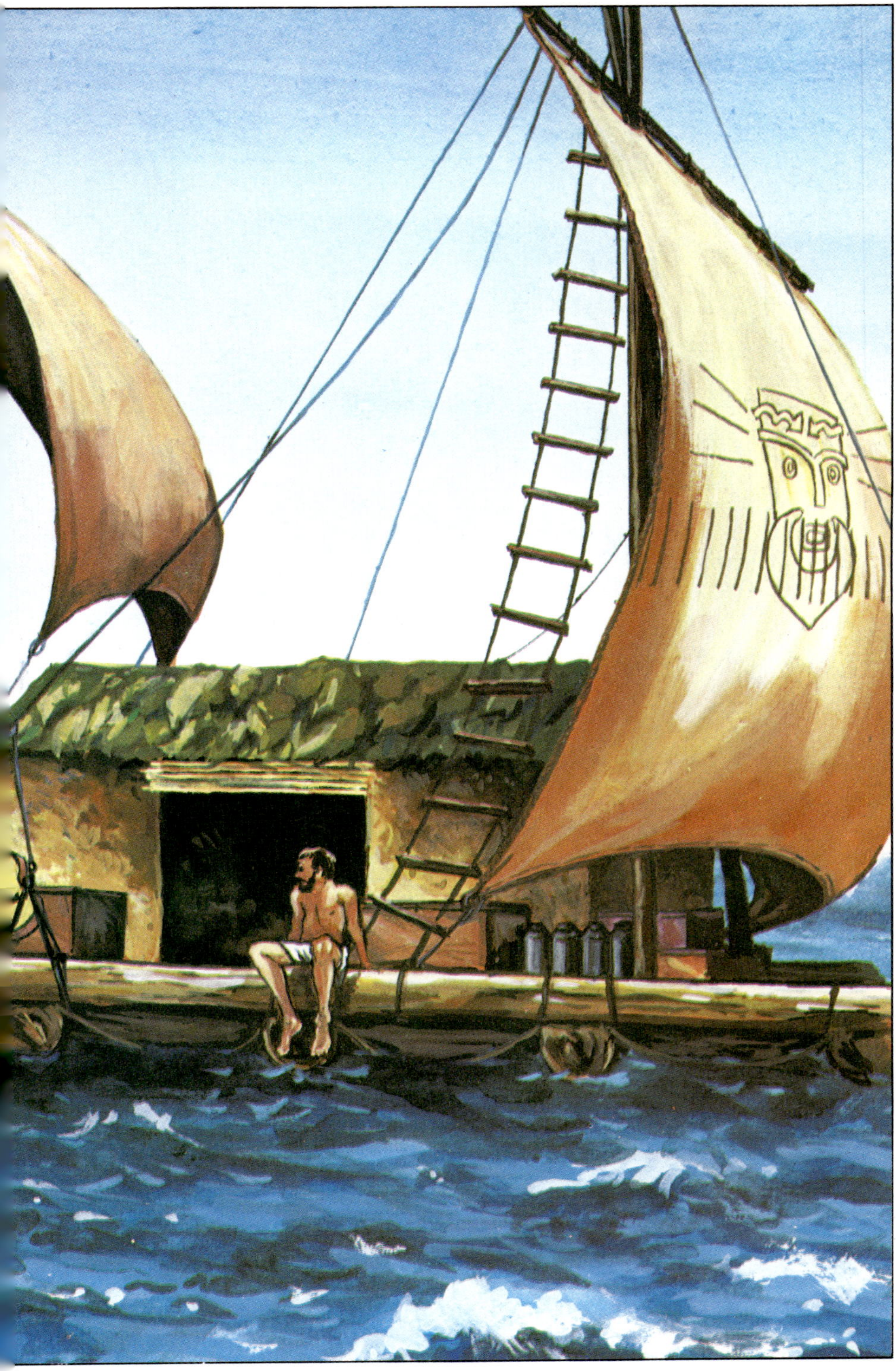

Late in the afternoon of the 97th day, they passed another island. Through a gap in a red coral reef they saw a blue lagoon. Along the shore of the lagoon, they saw people and palm roofed huts. Two people paddled an outrigger canoe out to meet them. One of the islanders said "Good night" as he shook the adventurers' hands. These were the only English words he knew. Later Knut went ashore with the islanders. They wanted him to stay, but he had to hurry back to the raft. The *Kon-Tiki* continued to drift along the coral reef.

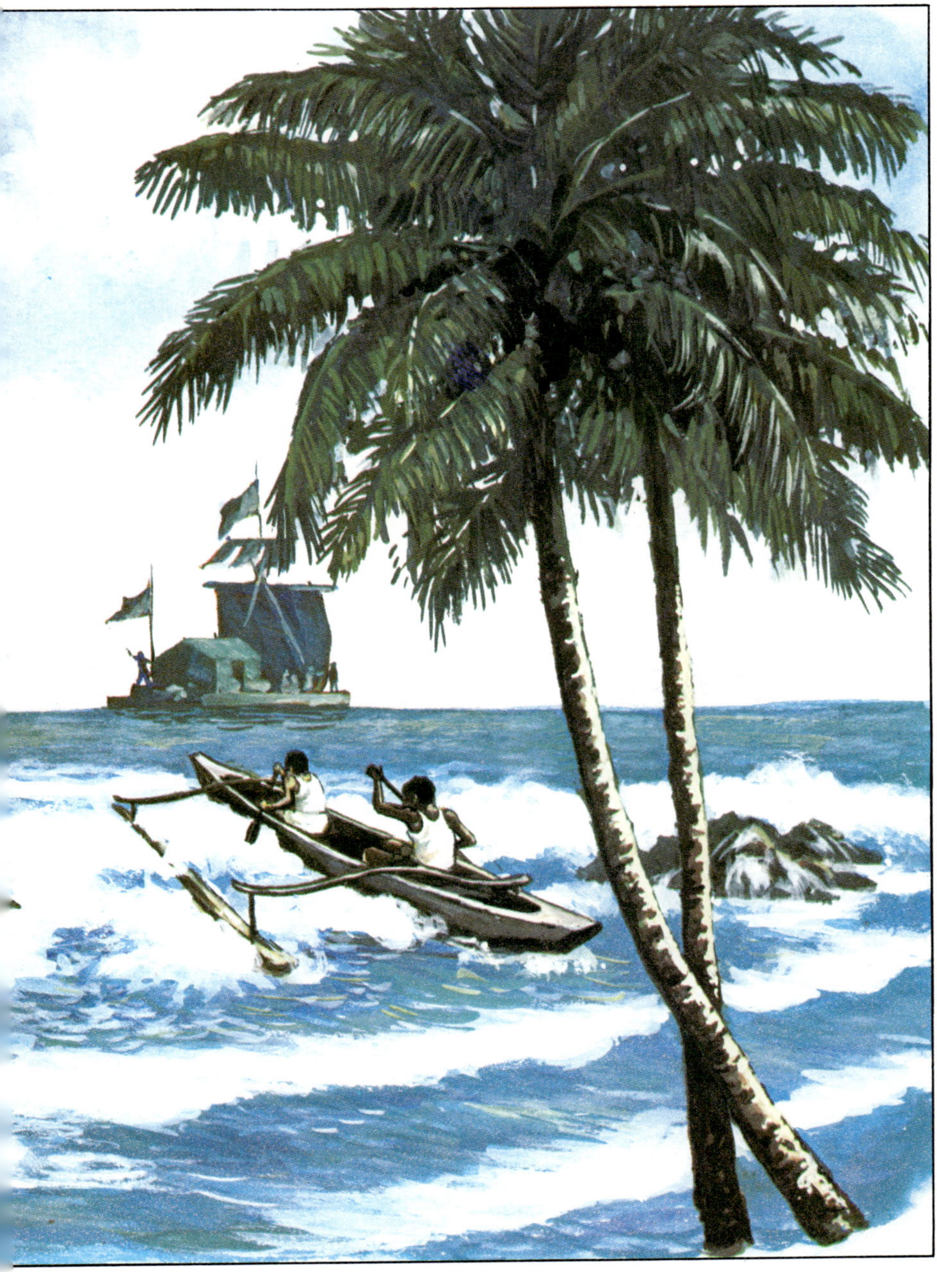

Great waves pounded the reef as the men prepared for a wreck landing. They spent several anxious hours as they were slowly carried towards the reef. They made contact with a radio operator in Rarotonga. Torstein told him that they were drifting towards the Raroia Reef. Their last message was, "OK. Fifty meters left. Here we go. Good-bye."

Then the swell caught them. Their anchor gave way and they cut it loose. On the crest of an enormous wave, the *Kon-Tiki* was dashed onto the reef. Within a few seconds, the raft was a shattered wreck. But no one was lost.

The men saved all that was valuable of their equipment, including a model of the raft made by Knut.

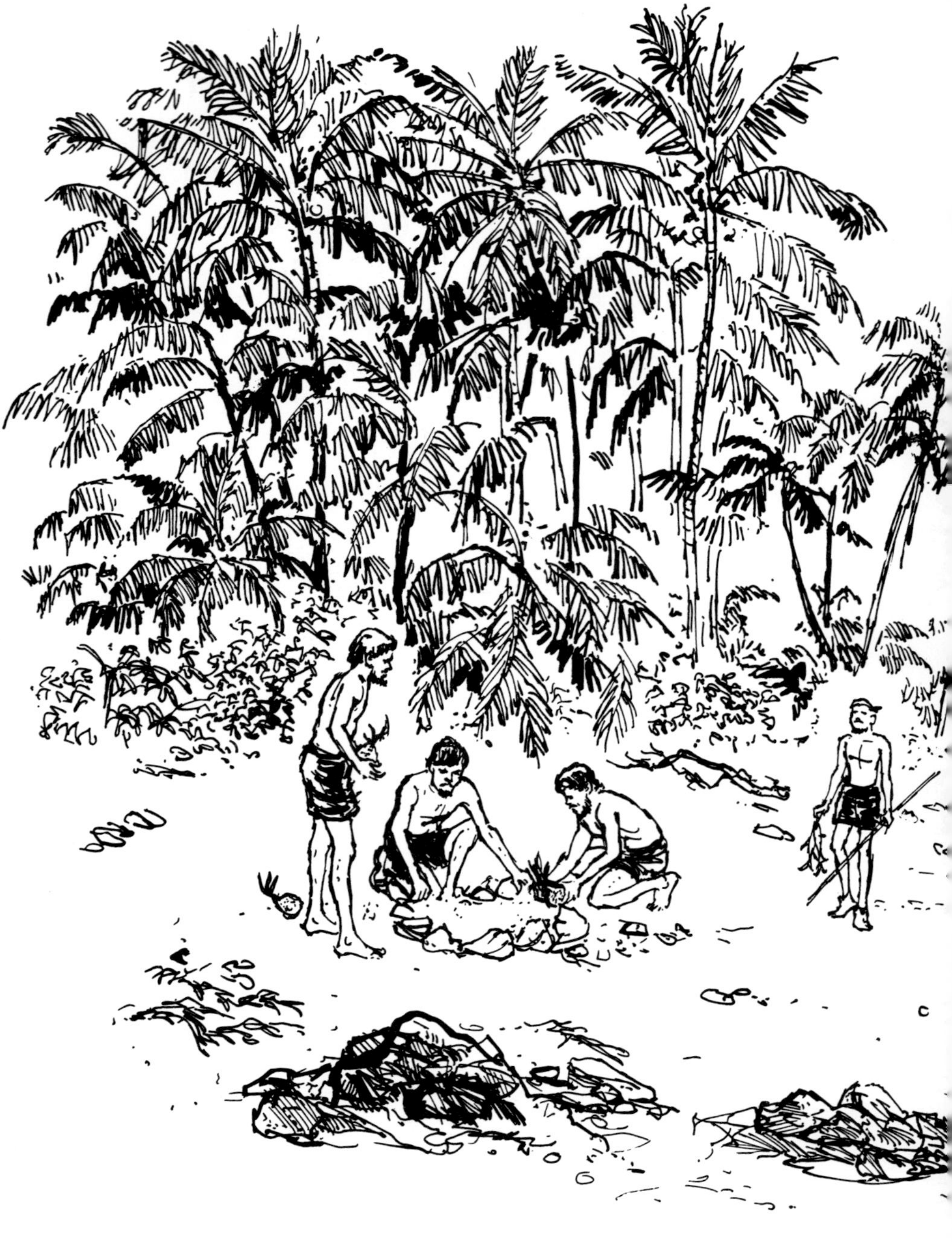

The crew spent the night on a small uninhabited island in the lagoon. After their radio transmitter dried out, they used power from a small hand generator to contact a radio operator. This radio operator thought the call was a fake. But finally, a man in Rarotonga heard them. After that everything went smoothly.

Before long, two outrigger canoes came from a nearby island. The crew of the *Kon-Tiki* got ready to leave the island. But first they planted a sprouting coconut they had brought from Peru. The next day they went in canoes to the larger island.

The islanders gave the crew of the *Kon-Tiki* a tremendous welcome. That night they enjoyed a tremendous feast. The Polynesians talked about the legend of how their ancestor, Tiki, had come over the sea many hundreds of years before. The adventurers told the tale of their voyage in the *Kon-Tiki*.

News of their safe arrival went around the world. The French schooner, *Tamara*, took the crew and the *Kon-Tiki* to Tahiti. The great adventure had ended successfully.

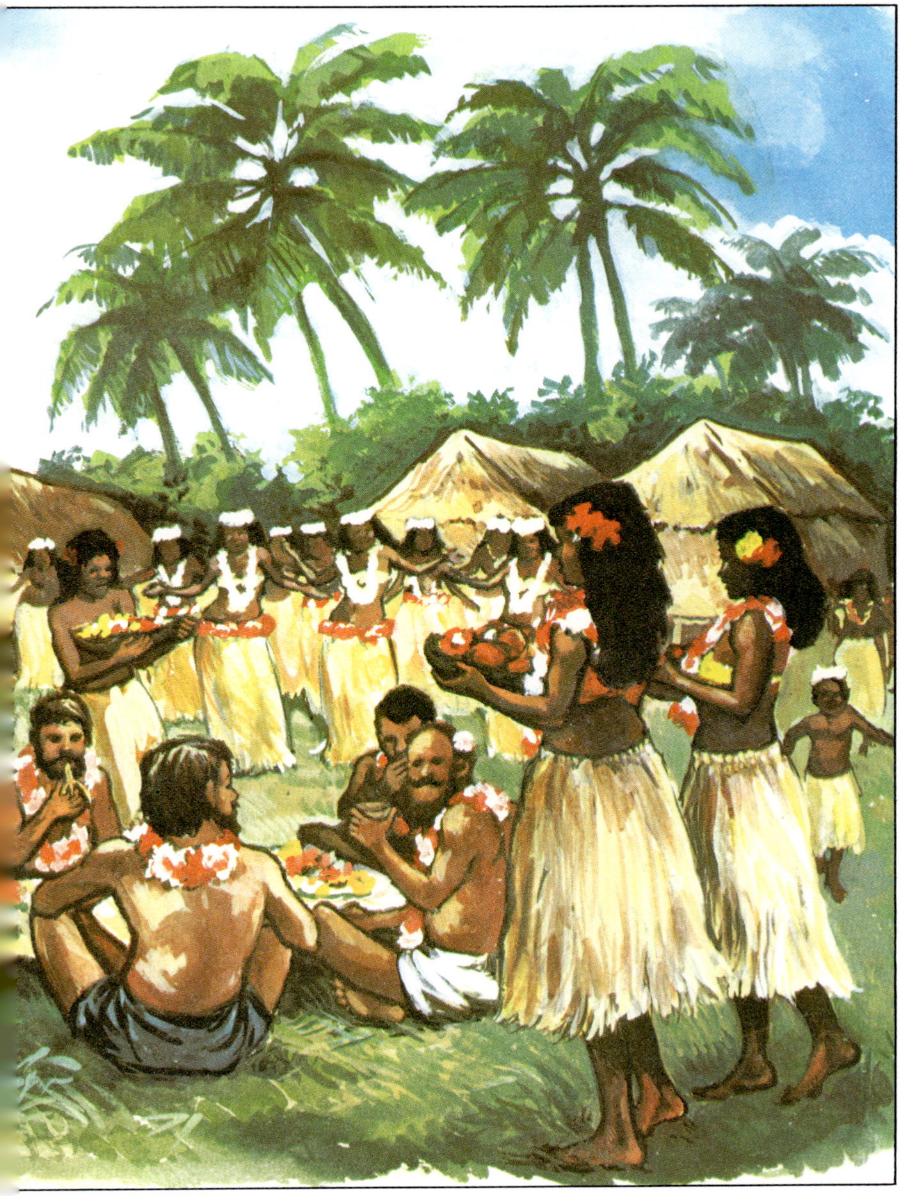